Best of
Manchester Poets

Volume 1

Puppywolf

Puppywolf
Manchester
United Kingdom
web: http://www.puppywolf.co.uk
email: enquiries@puppywolf.co.uk

First published June 2010

A catalogue record for this book is available from the British
Library.

ISBN 978-0-9565819-0-7

Contents

Foreword

Sneeze in Manchester and you'll infect a poetic genius, or two. The city that's England's creative capital is home to hundreds of poets: young, old, formally educated, informally educated, of all colours, creeds, genders and sexualities.

If there's one thing they have in common it's Mancunian bravado – the slightly insane give-it-a-go spirit that can get a person in trouble but every now and again produces something wonderful. There was a bravado explosion a few years ago, resulting in the Madchester music scene. And as the 21st century becomes firmly established, we might just be on the brink of another explosion, but this time with the written word.

The new Manchester poetry, which is collected here for the first time outside local zines, has a number of origins.

The scene is driven by the spoken word, via the many open mic nights spotted around the city. These are not the slam competitions so fashionable elsewhere but something far more relaxed and entertaining (and would you expect anything else from Manchester?). These nights showcase new writers, who are encouraged to get behind the mic and give it their best shot. Professionals and semi-professionals strut their stuff too.

Then there are the writing workshops. Forget about the worthy, low-key affairs found elsewhere. These are energetic brainstorms where talented poets spark from each other, exploring techniques and ideas. Such groups are everywhere, and it really is the case that people organize them with little more than the desire to help others.

The new poetry follows on from the Madchester scene, but it's possible to argue it's closer to stand-up comedy than music. Pills, thrills and kink sometimes feature, but at its heart (and we use that word advisedly) it's about people expressing how they live, and how they see the world. This is when the poetry is most successful, charming, and accessible.

The sacred forefathers for many Manchester poets are the Mersey Sound writers. However, there's a freedom of expression and individuality found in the Manchester scene that leaves behind even McGough, Henri and Patten. Their DNA is ours too, and we're thankful, but we've evolved significantly.

The poetry is rarely cynical or twisted. There's surprisingly little wretched wringing of hands. This isn't your father's poetry, and definitely not your grandfather's. Modern Manchester poets lean towards celebrating life, although they're fully aware this is a hard won privilege.

In the end, the new Manchester poetry is about having the confidence to express yourself, and not caring if you don't get away with it. It's not about righteous expression. It's about entertaining expression.

Enjoy it. It's powerful stuff. Infectious, even.

– *The editors (Manchester, June 2010)*

p.s. This book is by no means a definitive representation of Manchester poetry. To learn about future volumes of *Best of Manchester Poets*, sign up to our email newsletter at http://puppywolf.co.uk.

The poems

SHIRLEY PERCY

Manchester

I am the city.
Made by lives, I make lives;
come and see. Now, in the morning
I put on lemon light,
watercolour greys and placid pinks
over that wind dance of debris,
the significant trivia
left by feral teenagers whose howls
sliced the night; unaware that light exists
in them, they scrabbled for it
down dark holes.

Watch me luxuriate
in sunbeams; sprawl
stretching my extremities towards
those non-places existing
only on the way to somewhere
else. I breathe. I sigh.

Listen. Now trams trundle,
greet each other with mating cries.
Wearily the piano accordionist claims
her corner, Market Street/Portland Street.
Later her daughter will claim Piccadilly.
The mother settles, cossets
dark hands in skimpy shawl,
returns to ritual homeland tunes
incongruous here. Early workers
ignoring her reality, dash
into a handy sandwich shop, hear
not her melodies, but rhythms
of their imagined ticking clock.
You and I hear. Give her something.

Let us have a pound's worth
of her nostalgia.

Central library celebrates
the circle, opens its marble wedding cake
to bookworms, CD worms, play
peckers crowding like pigeons.
A young woman, jostled, snaps
shut her brisk brown briefcase,
leaves pit-patting on red high heels
towards her life goals. A shadow
slinks round to the job centre, hardly
hoping now to leave behind
his unmarked and devalued, oozing days.

St John Street; establishment calm
where medical specialists soothe anxiety
with opulence. Round the corner,
on Deansgate, crowds flood through me.
If we could speak body language, you and I
what would we hear from gestures
in the crowd? That pink old lady
flouncing her petticoats, is she still
sixteen? I too am young
and old. A passing musician's hand
shows rhythms from the Carmen
singing in his head. A high-booted
cowboy strides past in Stetson
and fantasies of freedom.
"Don't fence me in."

Yet darkness speaks in hunched
shoulders and the liquid life of the eyes.
Some, caught like flies on a meniscus
of trivia, thrash about for ease.
She walks seeing what is not. He tramps
his own mind corridors, stopped
blank walls that will not thin

to the light. Have these reached the end
of their story, their tether, their lives?
Not here. Such are secretly, hygienically
removed. No notice says "This tram stop
is for the dead only."

Sun melts into cloud. Showers
pelt me with rhythms. I smile
at the gleam sheen of wet
pavements, transparency showing me
in better light, the brightness
of another possible city shining through.

Evening comes. Teenagers
will wander again with the two-tiered
homeless, *Big Issue* sellers, sure
of a bed for the night, and the restless
rest. See, I am greeted
by clapping wing beats, bobbing and bowing,
comfortable coos. I welcome
my pigeons despite their red toes
tickling my roofs. They will roost
with me tonight, dozing for precious
seconds of city silence.

Farraday House

The foreground
has become their horizon.

Enough is to venture
from own flat to dining room,
a voyage fraught with obstacles
more stubborn and more solid
than furniture of yesteryear.
"Why are doors so hard to open?
Why are teapots so heavy here?"

"Because you're getting old, Annie
like the rest of us."

The particular, sieved
from general jumble, fascinates.
"These flowers look real, a beautiful
shade, and see, they even make
plastic water nowadays."

Awareness shortens;
the time tyrant is squashed
by a new perspective, demoted
to measuring the distance
between lunch and tea.

Tales of the past
become legends, recited
in unchanging ritual, to protect
against the multiplying mutations
going on outside.

Outside
can suddenly burst in.
With banshee wail, an ambulance
came for Margery, who fell
down the yawning chasm
between bed and table.

Real business
now, is barter. "Ethel swapped me
three fruit jellies for three
of my butter toffees."
"Who's got notepaper to write
to Margery in hospital?"

The unreal paraphernalia
of bank accounts, housing benefit,
attendance allowances,

is left to old children
still on the outside
whose own horizons
are beginning to close.

EMMA ROBINSON

December

She picked at the thread of her cardigan,

picked at it until it unravelled a little
until the exposed area began to get longer
teasing it between the thumb and forefinger
pulling, pulling, easing the wool away from the whole.

She was an expert picker, once she picked so hard
at a thread that she made her best friend cry.
She picked and picked and wouldn't leave
Clare alone about what went on at home.
She picked until there was nothing there.

She had often picked at her mother
if she'd been theirs from the start would
they've loved her more been kinder or fairer?
Would she have felt less alone and abandoned?
Her mother unwound between her fingernails.

She really picked with the man of her life
couldn't stop, got addicted
pulled at his clothes, his hair, his shoes
then at his intentions, promises, fidelity,
at last he began to spin away.
She held his last fibre in her yellow grasp
he disentangled in her hands.

Of course her daughter couldn't escape
the inching fingers clawed and snatched
with her nails and her teeth
digging, mangling her fabric loose;
her daughter unsnarled before her eyes.
She couldn't stop the picking and pulling
the tugging and heaving

the plucking and drawing
the jerking and hauling

a pile of wool, unravelled
kinked and warped
sits
at her bent and twisted feet
She tries to reach down
desperate to weave the pieces back together
but she's forgotten how to mend
if she ever knew how.

Until finally now, in December
it's cold out, cold in.

She sits in the kitchen and picks
at the wall- all alone

and she's nothing left to wear.

JACKIE HAGAN

A Made-up Town

You know the way parents don't get a handbook?
Well ours didn't have any books,
They had an accent, and an attitude.
So they made it up.
Our imaginary town.

I was the youngest,
And allowed to do whatever I liked.
But there was nowhere to go and nothing to do.
So this is my skill:

I could make a bag of no-frills crisps
My best mate for the day,
Call it Barry and love it to bits
And then eat it and go out to play.

I had eight imaginary friends.

Our parents didn't teach us right from wrong
In the same way
As the parents of kids I met when I left
My imaginary town.

They didn't teach us
How many continents there are
Or what continents are
Or what the point of knowing that is.

They didn't teach us about politics
But we felt its effects.
So when I left
It was hard to impress
The Other kids

The kids who grew up into adults who think it's clever
To laugh at peoples' spelling mistakes
And feel sorry for us cos we've never eaten
Some sort of shit food we don't care about.
Adults who 'can't believe!' we don't know something they
                                                        know,
When it's clear they don't know that much,
And they've learnt it all from books.
The words they use aren't their own.

On our island,
We couldn't give a crap about spelling.

I found whole worlds of cerise and electric blue
And brought them into our house in little cupped hands like
"Here, look what I found for you."

I'd adamantly dance my head off
For any audience,
I was just copying me mum.

My parents were young enough
And mad enough
To know exactly what I was on about
When I talked complete shit
About the people in the woods
And the fairies up my nose
About the bumdots and the pindits
Not humouring me, but joining in
With their own delicious twaddle
They hadn't finished being kids themselves yet.

We found new expressions every day
And cared so little and so much.
Cluelessly mismatching lifestyles and laughing
And laughing and laughing
At biscuits.

We could make a funfair on the landing
Using a chair, a sock and some Play-Doh.
Lick a slug for a laugh.
And get a Dad who's been at work all day
To do a forward roll
And mark him out of ten for it.

We didn't know what we were meant to be
So we just were.
The world wasn't there
To tell us we were wrong
We sung our own song so badly out of tune it was beautiful.
We spelt it so wrong it was beautiful.
We made an entire world out of nothing.

People Like Us

We don't see in black and white,
We dream in technicolored cabarets of multicoloured
                              shopping trolleys.

We know how savage hope is,
the incongruity of some chairs
and the magic mothers weave.

Need to leave the 9-5 for those it's for
and dress to the hilt
in beauty, disgust and cosmic dust.

We know that cup's wearing lippy cos it's getting ready for a
night on the town with Pat its best mate who's a whiskey-
                              drinking saucer.
We know how funny peas are (and that they're Geordies),
that curtains are eyelids,
and that people are people no matter what they're doing.

We know that apostrophes mean
fuck all,
we're easily enthralled and appalled.

Know there's a thousand billion sides to every story,
to every word,
to every intake of breath.

Know the reality and unreality of death.
We know how multi-coloured blue is,
How full-bodied grey is,
and the very differing personalities of the letters of the
                                                    alphabet.

We don't so much question, as know this answer's one of
                                                    many.

Know that words are just building blocks,
simple-minded shapes in primary school colours: toys.
That language is a framework
like holding water together.

See how strong the world tastes in our mouths?

We've always existed.

In our time been burnt as witches,
called empaths, shamans, gurus, stupid flighty bitches
deranged, frivolous, or hilariously – oblivious,

pernickety, irrational, over-sensitive, ridiculous,
perplexing, dyslexic, too intense and always wrong
and made to feel like we never belong,

been exploited, beaten, and electroshocked,
been kept in the attic, been mocked, forgotten,
Had our powers twisted by insistent psychiatrists
Or stolen by tablets, and tablets, and tablets,
Been patronised to shit, dismissed as fools
And had our wings shorn early, by the hell of school,

Bent and twisted out of shape we've flown inward and wilted
                                                    or soared

and if none of that,
then ignored

see how strong the world tastes in our mouths?

It's no wonder we really do talk to the moon

ROD TAME

I Know

I don't normally converse
about the nature of this universe.
Don't know if God ever existed.
But assuming that he did,
I think I know the way
he felt on that seventh day,
putting up his feet
to find his world complete,
like when you walked into mine.

In the time Paleolithic,
the buzz was terrific
when flint struck flint,
starting a fiery glint.
But no blazing bark
compares to the spark
when I touch your skin.

It is somewhat akin
to Armstrong's one small step.
Space-suited and booted,
he Earth-gazed amazed.
Bathing in your blue-eye hue,
I have an inkling of the twinkling
in that unique view.

Because I know how it felt,
when a Conqueror became king,
when the Wright brothers took wing,
when Alexander Graham's bell
went ring-a-ding-ding!
Even when Sinatra found his swing.
In other words...

Here is my historic win,
explaining this euphoric grin.

I know that
I am loved by you
and I know
I love you too.

Renaissance Man

In the beginning,
there was darkness.

In the Garden of England,
seeds of self-loathing,
sown by my Father,
fell on fertile soil.
Deep-rooted fear took hold.

Blessed Adam and Eve feasted,
gorged on lush fruit.
Cursed Adam and Steve starved,
denied earthly delights;
no serpent's temptation.
Sinless desires smouldered
in a personal hell
of peaceful obedience.

Neon Northern Lights
heralded a new dawn.
Venetian blinds pulled back,
revealed enlightened dancefloors.
Statuesque David
moved among fluorescent frescoes
with perfectly proportioned cherubim,
Mona Lisa smiling.

Venus rising
unafraid and unashamed
in a Queen's court of refracting colour.

Heart-reviving humanists
took to the stage,
faced the inquisitor's challenge,
"Dance or death?"
I danced.
Broke free from barbarian chains,
found a non-linear perspective,
and flourished in a heartland
of thirsty scholars.

Old World view shattered.
A thousand fragments of brilliance
reformed.
This man advanced.
Reborn.

DOMINIC BERRY

Oh, Aubergine!

Hint of mint.
Tongue tips glint.
We are... skint
– not broke.
She fixes me.
Woke me.
Clicks her tongs,
our ovens heat.
Oil sparks lash.
We have no cash.
I say, "It's OK,
love,
we'll make ends meet."
She says, "We make ends... veg!
And middle.
And... top."
I feel pressure drop.
Sauces slop,
thick then runny.

Our riches are greater than money.

Hint of mint.
Moroccan tagine.
Oh, l'amour!
Oh, aubergine.
Smoking nightshade.
Dark and lean.
Oh, l'amour!
Oh, aubergine.
She'll degorge
then stir my bean.
Oh, l'amour!

Oh, aubergine.
Lick her plates
all shiny clean.
Oh, l'amour!
Oh, aubergine.

Share this moment,
share this meal,
share the cost...
don't share how I feel.
Don't talk too sweet,
don't recollect.
But her eyes reflect
when we first met...

She was
Johnny Cage's shadow kick!
The silver smudge on Tricky's lip.
She was Nancy Boy, Kylie (with Nick),
Byker Grove – Noddy's kiss!
She was Skunk Anansie – "Weak As I Am",
she was the defence of Paul McGann,
Sonic's sneakers, Kate's Red Shoes,
Jean-Pierre Jeunet's sepia blues,
The Simpsons, back when they couldn't draw.
Kurt Cobain's comic pinned to a door.
Beered-up, singing Cohen's words,
"I've seen The Future, baby.
It is murder."
She was an Army of Me,
tough vegan machine.
Oh, l'amour!
Oh, aubergine.

Then –
she married.
He doesn't cook!

Yet, our time
he so easily took.

She is hot veggie quiche!
He is cold flan.
She's olive paella.
He's beans from the can.
She's full Sunday roast.
He's lettuce and dips.
She's cranberry roulade.
He's yesterday's chips.
He's king of the noodles.
She's strawberry cake queen.
Oh, l'amour!
Oh, aubergine.
His celery's wilted.
She's luscious and green.
Oh, l'amour!
Oh, aubergine.

Don't talk too deep.
Don't share how I feel.
Occasionally, share
a meal.
Hint of mint.
Tongue tips glimmer.
Smile,
make a hearty dinner.
Nothing else.
Don't act too keen.
Oh, l'amour!
Oh, aubergine.

Share this moment,
lush. Serene.
Oh, l'amour!
Oh, aubergine.

Trying to Remember

I am trying to remember
there's a day that's going to be,
when I won't sit with silence sat
so clammy next to me.
I am trying to remember
there's a day that I will find.
It's beneath the swollen grin
of my slack window blind.

I am trying to remember
that one day I will go out.
I will push through the burly noise
that knocks the street about.
And I am trying to remember,
though this fact I'll have to check,
that you can go out here and not get
a knife in your neck.

My confidence is hungry
like my empty shelves.
I am trying to remember
bread and beans don't buy themselves.
Silence listens slowly,
chews skin around my thumb.
I am trying to remember
there's a day that's going to come

when I'll go back to the shop
and no longer see the knives
glinting in the check out girl
and lorry driver's eyes.
I am trying to remember
that I will feel safe, one day,
and yet, each night, it feels like
that day's getting further away.

CATHY BRYANT

In a Class of My Own

One of the most dreadful of my disabilities
Was to be raised middle class.
(That's 'clarse' to rhyme with 'arse',
Not 'class' to rhyme with 'lass'.)
In our detached (very detached) house;
The Guardian every day and two French cars
Willow trees in the garden
Aspirations in the stars.
Not that the working classes
(or lower classes) weren't *marvellous*.
Some are even bright enough
For Further Education (not Higher);
When you meet them, don't treat them
Any differently.
Their ignorance isn't their fault
(pronounced *fawlt* not *folt*).
Some of my best friends were
working class.
Then we came North.
Then we came North, to a poor village.
'North of Manchester', we were told.
'Scotland?' we asked.
'No, there's some England
North of Manchester but not quite Scotland.'
'That far North? Good Lord!
Good Lord!' exclaimed mother
(that's 'Mother', never 'Mum'),
'It'll be all flat caps and eeh bah gum.'
So we moved and I was very scared
of the savages we'd find, for whom I felt
singularly unprepared.
And we came North, and I fell in love.

I fell in love with people who didn't gush
Who were OK with flaws
Who said good stuff was 'lush'
And who'd fight for a cause.
At home I was told off
For saying 'skewel' instead of 'skoowl',
Swimming 'pewel' instead of 'poowl'.

Decades later in a Parisian queue
To see Matisse at the Pompidou
I was accosted by fellow Brits.
They were very Southern and
quite clearly all true blue.
As we spoke they observed sadly,
'Your vowels do have a northern taint',
(In their ghastly cut-glass accents,
oh how quaint, how quaint, how quaint.)
I'd never felt so proud as my smile became cold.
To me a 'taint' of Northern-ness
Is joy, is truth, is gold.
I tried not to think of them
As posh Southern gits,
Those snobbish Brits,
As a wave of homesickness hit me
For my best mate calling me a daft a'porth,
For proper chips and polemic,
And cheerful faux gem glitz.
Flowers in Fletcher Moss,
A place I love and where I fit.
And back here,
home in my beloved Manchester,
I laughed hollowly
at my prejudices old and new;
Remembering, as we used to patronise
The workers, the 'lowers',
How we sneered too at the 'uppers',

Those public school aristocrats
(With better titles than ours),
Who, unlike us, don't you know,
Had such a false and twisted social perspective.

The Poetry Diet – Drop a Stanza in Just Two Weeks!

Breakfast is blank verse spread with ballads
Or a bowl of elegy and a boiled ode.

For lunch, try a rondelet with herbs such as cento.
Follow with a lay if liked,
Sweetened artificially if necessary.
Vary your cinquains and quatrains
According to season.

For dinner a well-grilled villanelle
With a simple side sonnet and a little steamed prose.
Do beware of prose. It can be hard to stop.
Make sure to keep crunchy acrostics to hand.

For snacks, try haiku.
They're surprisingly meaty
And will satisfy.

Free verse is unlimited.

Drink at least eight couplets a day,
And up to three glasses of freshly-squeezed phrases.

When tempted by fizzy limericks,
Chewy clerihews, chocolate epics and sweet lyrics,
Visualise yourself as a sexy sestina
Rather than doughy doggerel.

This poem is scientifically proven
And has been approved by dactyls
And other members of the metrical profession.
It really, really works.

Vanessa Fay

'Chav'

Crumpled cigarette packets
are her pockets of magic
as she thumbs them
with yellow tinged fingers
leopard print eye flickers on Fenstow road

she's too old for small school
and big school doesn't want to know
not enough room
for her big head
and miniscule
self-confidence, jaded
short battered skirt, faded
sprouting awkward scrawny bruised legs
if you could see the grime that coats the inside of her head

gets her nose pierced
stings... she likes it
gets it pierced with a gun
and her grin screams, she likes it
scratches but underneath stinks
and however hard she tries
the world refuses to vanish when she blinks

she knows how to make her gutsy walk talk
defy cars and traffic lights
but not quite conquered how to get through the night
so she just tries and squeezes tight
puts on her best swagger

knows the smack of back-handed thank-yous
and how it feels to queue

without harbouring any clue of a future
day-in
day-in

knows under the cockiness there's not much else but
self-doubt
and that she's alone

doesn't want to be
wants to have the soft curve of a hand on her arm
wants to know how that feels
but too busy fighting shadows

texts friends
she's made up
500 mates on Facebook
but doesn't know a soul
knows how much she's worth in a buy and sell
and that her hope is going to hell
so might as well
drown it while she's here
in Spar's cheapest beer
mixed with Ribena

'coz she's not, and was never allowed to be,
one of those student dreamers
knows the true sweat of the streets
knows how she tries to hide
how hard her heart beats
when she's playing tough
but all they call her is 'chav'
'rough'
knows she doesn't own a name.

Outspoken

Disarmed, ready
with sisters
that I never had
we line in height order
disordered, manic, sad
and roar!
angrier than stomach pain

we are kettles reaching boiling point
have no individual names
we are collected, packaged
the ground does not crumble beneath our feet
instead, it is as if the earth itself begins to beat
in time with our motion

for they may have stripped us
but never of our emotion
we are ravenous, feeling
thankful for this
we dance
dance like we have no other choice
we *can* dance
dance like it is our voice
expressive, loud, longing

outspoken
when we laugh
it is like the sun smacking the sky
diamond-knuckled
explosive, expansive
our hope
silver, succulent
frenzied, vehement
our hands
wild, wicked?

we do not take orders
we thrash out
tumble, fall
whirl, whizz
swallow up whole their doubt
lights flash in our eyes

outspoken
we take one another's hand tenderly
hold on with strength, ability, spirit
none of us say it
we just stand
shoulders brushing

meanwhile, suits push keyboard letters
write in standard English
what sounds wrong, harsh
splinters tongues
we are "abnormal,
sick, pained, insane...
[we] are not the same"

and yes, we outspoken
do not fit the shadows
we do not contort ourselves
instead, we bend
like spectacular fireworks.

CHRIS DOMMETT

Alice

Alice lay down the looking glass,
spread out the sherbet,
pulled out a razor
and began to cut from above.

No blood was spilt
but the nostrils were raw,
staring into reflections
of a depressant grin so Cheshire.

The world was brought to life,
rushes of blood beat in the brain,
all was so vivid
though almost surreal.

A cup of tea
sits before her,
but this is a party,
she wants the madness.

A crawling caterpillar
produces smoky image rising as it crawls,
familiar opium smells
comfort the mind.

She felt so big and so tall
as if she had grown immensely,
not expecting the residual effects
that soon were to come.

Loving this high
that would only last for minutes,
playing poker on the table
afraid of the ace of spades.

Her opposition
look identical,
unable to distinguish
between faces of randomly appearing twins.

Now distanced reflections
are detached from the present,
departed to another time,
tripping back to the magic of wonderland.

STEVE O'CONNOR

BMW

Straight man turns forty in a paper party hat
Aboveboard, mod-shirted
Razor-cut hair square to his accurate collar
Follows pub politics for more than kicks
Smears his words with casual bigotry
And has never kissed his son
Knows what the back of his hand is for
And has never kissed his son
Works diligently for his holidays
Can detail a day-by-day scam
Proper good with engines
'Like every man should be'
Will see you right for your MOT
And your wife
Calculates his smile
Brims with guile
Wouldn't mind a night in Styal Women's Prison
Wears derision like a fat man wears Speedos
And wears Speedos in all his sun-kissed photos
Sunburned onto your retina
Talks tenderly of his Angelina
The multi-coloured Ford Cortina
He drove at seventeen
Leather jacketed, pay-packeted cruiser
Lean leans to lean over and topples with girth
Inevitable with age
As sure as earth scatters across coffin lids
His kids will never go without
Won't learn from what it means to have nowt
And treasure those memories
Three times away to parts unknown each year
Fears queers

Likes bikes
And time apart from the wife
Seems to live a life of rosy-cheeked
Strictly white male bonding
And falling on the sword
And other such pursuits manly men get up to
When they're bored.

Grace

Grace can think in bullet-time
Throw a thought around and make you duck
Before it hits you
Beats up stuff until it works
Has been known to go berserk
Makes mirrors flinch and pinch themselves
Awake in her reflection
Gives water an erection
And with one swing of her hips
Shadow-bound spiders fall to their knees and worship

Grace is smooth and intense
White chocolate-dipped honeycomb out of the freezer
Turns burns to ice-cold showers
And knows the difference between heat and warmth
Will not explain what you don't know
So don't ask
She'll tease out your story
She's read every book on life-drawing
Draws breath that tastes of red wine kisses
And colours not yet invented

Grace is daft
Has the kind of laugh found at funfairs
Only ever uses two swear words
Uses both to power her ray gun
Bubblegum pop laser beams

Knickers ride up the bum of this anime ASBO angel
High-kicking her own battle of the planets
Never plans – but can read tea leaves
Gets the future – so she doesn't have to
Will one day speak Japanese – maybe

Grace wrote the book
On what it means to touch and be touched
And how to cut the bullshit
Totally uninhibited in her charm
Disarms you with a glance
Can't dance, can't sing – wrote a song about it
For her book
Cooks in the bedroom, fucks in the kitchen
So much more than a bewitching tease
One day she'll teach me Japanese

JOHN TOGHER

Piccadilly

I meet you
at the statue
on the hour
and think of
the drowning grip
I have on your face.
Your onion seed
eyes are ablaze.
I sigh, watch
the feathered clouds

disconnect above us.
You give a tug
on my sleeve,
"We're a clumsy version
of a good idea,
like pterodactyls."
I freeze-frame,
see you entwined
in bringing defeat,
deaf to my melancholy.
I stare at the chip
in your front tooth.

A Chance Meeting After a Ten Year Absence

She holds a rosary in her hand
yet keeps the devil up her skirt.
She picks the hours of least interruption
to dip her feet in the colours of the earth.
He thought himself a king,
holding a secret royalty in his chest;

with the depth of his heart a kingdom
and the curls on his head a crown.

She sees him walking towards,
and a faint recognition ignites.
He hasn't a clue but is drawn to her eyes.

She calls out, 'If you are who I think you are,
I've always wanted to make love to you.'

'Well, who do you think I am?' he replies,
remembering his social chameleon tendencies.

Rosie Lugosi

Queer Thanksgiving (With Special Thanks to William S. Burroughs)

Thank you for history.
For Queen Victoria and half of us wiped from existence.
Mary Whitehouse and jail-term blasphemy.
James Anderton and the swirling cesspits of our own making.

Thank you for religion.
For Christianity, Judaism, Islam,
Buddhism, Scientology, Mormons;
For all those who use their God's laws to hate.
Thank you for *Praise God for Aids* banners.
For *Gay Plague.*

Thank you for politicians.
Especially Margaret Thatcher and Section 28,
and all those who shied away from its repeal.
Thank you for Communism:
for we are bourgeois revisionist deviant scum.
Thank you for Fascism:
for we are pinko commie weirdo deviant scum.
Thank you for *scum.*

Thank you for psychology:
She must have been abused;
Too close to his mother;
It's the parents' fault;
Must have had a bad time with a man.
It's just not *natural.*
They shouldn't work with children.
They can choose.

Thank you for vocabulary:
for shirt-lifter, fudge-packer, shit-stabber,
bull-dyke, faggot, fruit, lezzie,

rug-muncher, turd-burglar,
bumboy, poofter, willy woofter,
pervert, predator, queer,
for *Too ugly to get a man,*
what she needs is a real one,
unnatural, diesel, man-hater, deviant, paedo.
Thank you for giving us two choices:
camp queen or butch lezzer.

Thank you for *It's Adam and Eve, not Adam and Steve.*
For *Are you Arthur or Martha?*
Thank you for the obsession with what we do in bed.
For top-shelf hot girl-on-girl action porn.

Thank you for telling us it would all be so much easier
if we just kept things quiet. Didn't scare the horses.
Stayed in the closet.

Thank you for burning us at the stake
Declaring us illegal, breaking us with hard labour.
Thank you for the Pink Triangle.
Thank you for beheading us in Saudi,
hanging us in Iran,
forcing us into marriages we don't want
in Islamabad and Burnley.
For bombing our pubs,
knifing us on Clapham Common.
For grinding us into the tarmac
of the world's school playgrounds.

Thank you for trying to douse our pride.
For giving us crumbs, for making us grateful.
For persuading those of us who are white and rich
that the battles have all been won.
Thank you for never going away.
Thank you for making us strong.
Thank you for our history.

We are writing our own future.
Thank you for keeping us on our toes.

Celebrity

These days, I can afford servants to light
the match for my huge cigar. When I'm tired of punching
cars they clean my nails
with steam-shovels. I have people to scratch my armpits,
wipe my backside, zip me up when I'm done.

All they're interested in are red carpet moments,
when my hands are the size of lions, hairy
and bad-tempered. My thumbs suck
sky out of mirrors, spit it
underfoot. Magnesium ghosts
flare my eyes to green. I can't tell them
how my bed still itches with beetles.

DERMOT GLENNON

What the Cosmos Sings to Me

Were I to annotate only what the cosmos sings
while dreaming my dreams of these absolutes
by kerbs of pavements to garden-fronted terraces
parked Allegros Fiats Fords
in phrases that don't mean a thing or "things"
yomping homeward hands on newsprint brisk in manner
unmeant smiles or nods or paper held high in salute
teaspoons of boiled egg for breakfast
tidy triangles of toast set square on side plates
tut tut mail strike immigrants murders
and somewhere in the distance Neptune orbits
but this is not what the cosmos sings to me
Joseph Emily get your shoes on
as the little Highland Terrier looks down
Susan Susan always called Susan or something similar
nondescript with overbite
the universe sings the song of swings
slides seesaws and dog mess bins
where council grass and tarmac meet and kiss
filling family Tax Credits and small horizons
spectacles and waiting rooms
the long dark march to baldness
in slow post office queues where tax discs can be paid
got to keep the spirits up but never let them soar
and Susan Susan always there's a Susan
each man has a Susan and Susan is a chore
and mail strikes murders one wonders why one bothers
and the cosmos sings of Susan and one doesn't anymore:
you've lost that loving feeling
Oh! Oh! That loving feeling
you've lost that loving feeling

but you've gained
two
stone
and discovered God discovered gods goblins
chakras crystals Wicca or whatever
and become routine and scheduled
a number line of dates and anniversaries
to be pencilled and observed like fourteen oblique oh-two
if you're lucky it's one hundred minutes pleasure
several months security twenty years inertia
twenty years of fear and there behind the roman blinds
at the scag end of the causeway are the civil and divorce courts
and it's either there or here
were I to annotate only what the cosmos sings
under the drippy concrete bridges
where the rain soaks jewels glinting
between the deep prophetic scribbles
of phrases that don't mean a thing or things
but catch the fragile light like stars
in dreams of somewhere far
of somewhere far away
far from here
far from computer spares shops
whose windows have a grill
decaying plastic over metal crazing cream or off-white squares
and oh Christ al-frigging-mighty
God it's all so bloody boring
like a Colin from next door
who's leaning up against his Qualcast
and talks incessant dullness
like a valid second language
as the flap of spring-fresh meadow-scented
clothes blows on an urban northern wind
and horizons narrow in the red-bricked rain-greyed grimness
of it all

Untitled

When I asked you to marry me
I think I liked your hair and skin
but now the former's like straw
and the latter's wearing thin
and your eyes were nice –
I really liked your eyes –
but they soon went and I'm
looking at the window reflected on glass
as if your soul retreated in

I used to like your hair and skin
it's why I asked you to marry me
but skin soon rots and your hair's like straw
and I think they were all I loved you for
but you are still here
in an odd sort of way
you pervade the house that we shared together
your smell still reeks through the house
it reminds me of your laughter and
smiles and everything

have I said I liked your hair and skin
it's why I asked you to marry me
and I liked your eyes
because you had nice eyes
but your eyes dropped out
and your skin is rotten
I still love you though and I haven't forgotten
the way you looked on our wedding day
with your hair all brushed
and your eyes all moist
and I look at you now; what a terrible waste
but although you're old, your waist's still thin

I think I liked your hair and skin
when I asked you to marry me

I think that's what I loved you for
though the latter's thin and the former's straw
things are different now and I love you more
as we sit and share the silence
equally between us
in the stillness of the attic
where you slowly rot to dust
propped up in the chair
dressed in your wedding dress
I wrap the blanket round you
to keep the warmth and moisture in

I used to love your hair and skin
but now I love you so much more
'though your skin is dry and your hair is straw
and I liked your eyes
because you had nice eyes
but I'll take them out because the lids don't close
and you used to get such bad night terrors
like the ones you got on the night you died
before I sponged you down with formaldehyde
and brought you here to the attic
from where your smell pervades my house
with a rickety bed to lay you in
where I still make love with your hair and skin.

STEPH PIKE

Age 7

it was the year of that dress;
a lemon-meringue mess
of yellow nylon
and white lace trim

in that dress
she was not the girl
who bent a paper-clip
and felt the whip of your hand
on her face

in that dress
she was not the girl
who threw her first punch
and heard the satisfying crunch
of her sister's nose

in that dress
she was not the girl
you chased with a belt
and who, for the first time,
smelt her own fear

in that dress
she was not the girl
who disappointed your days
with her strange
and awkward ways

in that dress
she was all things nice
sugar and spice
her mother's pride
the apple of her daddy's eye

in that dress
she was straight-jacket calm
good as gold
with folded arms and knees closed
who tried and tried to please

she was your bees knees

that was the year;
a little girl
in a bile-yellow dress
waiting to explode

Day Trippers

gulls shriek
we burst onto the seafront
hearts juddering like bus engines
laughing, we shovel crisps into
mouths too ravenous to shut
against the blowing sand

blue melts into yellow
the end of the summer
washes our backs with warmth
and your fingers rippling my hair

later, you dribble alien
words and someone else's
half-eaten spring roll into my ear
and I know we're
on the slow train home
half-cut, and happy

ANDREW OLDHAM

Why Guns Will Never Be Legal in England
(For Billy Collins)

Every time the sun is out
My neighbour has a barbeque
And invites all his family

They are loud

I try to drown them out by singing
My wife sings and the dog we never bought, sings
And the neighbours join in with tubas

They are louder

I go outside to the bottom of the garden
But I smell the burgers on the grill
Hear the yells and arguments amongst the onions

Louder still until they vibrate and

Everyone in my neighbour's garden splits
Like amoebae, identical division that speeds up
Two, four, eight, sixteen men flipping burgers

Louder still amongst the smoke

Two, four, eight, sixteen women screeching
Keep out of the road, get off that wall, don't do that
Their growth pushes down the garden fence

Louder still they move in

They now have barbeques in my cupboards
Divide in my bathroom and bung up plug holes
And sit on the dog we never bought
Louder still in the kitchen amongst the pans

Their children divide in our drainpipes
The continuous barbeque smoke drives out the spiders
In the end we move out and leave no forwarding address

The Calling of Young Tony

*"If you would be perfect, go sell all you have, give to the poor
and come follow me." (Matthew 19:21)* *

When he told his family the sky was falling, no one believed
                                    him
even when he dragged black clouds across the kitchen floor.
His mother tutted, washed them and flattened them in the
                                    mangle,
they hung on her washing line until Christmas and she gave
                                    them to neighbours.
Still wet, they flopped through letterboxes for the entire month
                                    of December,
rotted on hall carpets and mutely fired electric bolts at
                                    televisions.

When he brought the poor in during television adverts, his
                                    mother shooed
them from her parlour; he watched their tracks left behind on
                                    the linoleum floor.
Charcoal footprints that reminded him of dance diagrams,
                                    mapped out waltzing.
He told them lies and they took from the kitchen in the dead of
                                    night; his father called it theft.
Some built cars out of baked bean tins; some made soldiers
                                    from takeaway menus,
some built petrol bombs out of milk bottles and dropped them
                                    on their neighbours.

When he told his mother he could see, she blinded him with
                                    detergent.
So he used a fishing rod for a cane and tapped his way down
                                    the hall, humming blindly.

No one heard the front door shut and no one saw his face as he
pulled out the penny whistle.
Hook and rod over shoulder, he blew and blew but knew
nought of music or sound,
But still the lost followed him; the fools sang in his wake and
smiled with silent faces.
And all walked out of town into the closing horizon leaving
dance in their wake.

* St Anthony took this advice as a personal invitation addressed
to him by God at the age of 18.

RACHEL DAVIES

Pink Docs

Turning fifty she first noticed the change; a subtle
passing in the street without a word, an eye glancing
off her, a question unanswered.

By fifty five, unseen by the entire crew, she was able to spend
an afternoon watching an episode of *Life on Mars*
being filmed. She appeared in the episode, where Sam
last sees his mum. You can just about make her out
going round the bend.

At fifty six she robbed a bank; police are looking
for a man in his early twenties in grey hoodie and Raybans.

By fifty seven she could pass unnoticed
among home supporters at Eastlands, sporting a Nani shirt,
shouting 'Come on you Reds'.

At fifty eight she climbed to the top of the Manchester Eye
with a banner that read 'Supergran, the Invisible Force',
the slogan she painted in scarlet on the Town Hall wall.
It was left to the rain to wash it off.
Nothing was reported in the press.

At fifty nine, on Halloween, she danced naked in Albert
                                        Square,
passed over by the revelling undead.

Turning sixty she felt herself fading from reflections in shop
                                        windows,
appeared to walk through walls, was overlooked in shopping
                                        queues.
It was the last straw when a young man sat on her lap on the
                                        bus,
was deaf to her pleas to find another seat, just stayed put
to the end of the line.

She bought pink Docs on the internet.
She wears them hoping she'll be noticed
falling through the cracks in pavements.

Whit Friday

They march along in haphazard platoons,
these happy militias, loud and proud
in blue uniforms with red lapels, festooned
with gold braid. Passing the beer-slaked crowd

they march in step, as far as their twisted brass
will allow, setting their feet down to the sound
of the drummer beating the steady bass
of a Sousa tune. The revellers mill around

the edge like butterflies about a buddleia,
with glazed eyes, cheering their favourite bands,
their voices oiled by Theakstons. The biggest cheer
is for a tuba player who can't free up her hands

to catch her wind-blown score. One player,
a Casanova in his youth, holds his euphonium
as he used to hold a woman, as if a prayer
were in his arms around her curves and some

erotic spell in his fingers playing at her valves.
His lips blow promises into her throat, his tongue
moistens her mouthpiece like a tender salve.
Her coquettish brass bell laughs as they march along.

The trumpeter triple-tongues *Abide With Me*
while the trombone slides, a fingerpost to heaven.
The ale and music flows over Saddleworth Moor
like the Holy Ghost, like a Pentecostal blessing.

GERRY POTTER

Planet Middle Age

Hold your horses
Your beer
Hold all
That you hold dear.
Hold your heart up to the sky
Hold your tongue
Until language turns to imagery.

I'm up and around all this
All over it
Turned inside out like a well-worn midnight.
Hackneyed.
Journeyed till the return is boring.
Heat-seeking.
I'm seeing things in all their jaundiced glory.
There's got to be a better cliché
Than going bald and grey.
Than the dawn of a brand new day.

I'm the old rock'n'roll
Made now.
A shining tick-tock
Winding down from the romantic Eighties.
And we all say in unison
Like lemmings
Eloquent lemmings
Middle-age is the new young.
We don't say in unison
I'm frightened.
We don't tell the truth.
We are the curse of positivia
The dreams of insomnia.

Planet Middle Age
And all its aliens
Are meant to be wise and friendly.
Phases on stunning.
Is there life on Mars?
Is there any truth in the rumour
That you're still as weak as a kitten
Shaky as a blossom on a tree?
Planet Middle Age
And all its aliens
Are meant to be strong and tall
Green.

It's the goodbyes
that ache
Willow-dappled echoes
Of echoes long gone.
Up to the sky
Hidden in clouds if you please.
If there's a special place where echoes rain
Then build me a house with a leaky roof.
Get me a cat I can tell secrets to
And let it pour
And let it purr.

My sister in law
Was the last of her family
My home town a dream.
Have I seen all there is?
Been all there is?

Planet Middle Age
And I'm not tuned into
Its frequency.
Or matured into its delicacy.
All a bit fast
This slowing down
Growing old.

I'm old
In love
And young.
Old
Young
Growing
And middle-aged.

The Witherers

Pokey dark fingery
Thingery
Spindly men and women.
Woodcuttings and real.
They stand corner stood
Whittling maggots from tears.
Stand corner stood
Stealing twinkles
From eyes
Leaving you dimly lit with malady.
Blights and monsters.
Beware The Witherers
Their disguises
Sometimes they look like
Friends.

Witherers hover two inches outside your window
Echo tap footsteps.
Pollute your dreams
Steal beauty sleep
Stuff it in jars
And a-down they go
A-withering
A-quivering
A-selling it in pubs for a fiver.

Dark they go
Seeping
Sagging
Slobbering the putrid of drains.
Beware The Witherers
Their disguises
Sometimes they look like
Family.
Down they go
Working underground and overtime
Creeping around the graveyard shift.
Check your mother's fingernails
For coffin splinters
Check her breath for a rose scent
Or a lily breeze
And her purse for the acquisitive
Scuffed souls of children.

Never let them tell you secrets
A Witherer's secret could steal your soul
Make you murder your angel.
"Snap her wings, garrotte her with her halo.
Rip out her feathers."
They rasp,
Whisper tinny.
Witherers hate wings.

The Witherer will sell you your heartbeat
Read the untellable in your mind
And broadcast it to the world.
They'll invisible in the corner
Staring at your favourite chair.
That chill that grabs your spine?
A Witherer's stare that is.
Dark they go.
Beware The Witherers and their disguises
Sometimes they take on your features.

Sometimes take on your future.
Sometimes they look like your furniture.
A lumpy cushion could be a Witherer's knees.
Witherers have knobbly needs.

Never join a Witherer's song
Their melodies mame.
It's the howl in your pipes
Calling your name.
An owl song sung by a demon.
Witherers thirst for and feast on the last death rattle
The almost of breath
Nibble at grief
Bleed bad medicine
Slow poison
Exalt mediocre
And dark they go.
Beware The Witherers and their disguises
Sometimes they look like your doctor.

If you see a Witherer in the silver of a mirror nod your head
three times, touch your heart and say 'love'.

Angela Smith

After Midnight

1:00 am
has smudged mascara,
clutches an open bottle of champagne
and a half-eaten kebab
with extra chillies.
Turns on the telly,
changes channels sixteen times
and turns it off again
without so much as a by-your-leave.
Makes you laugh till the champagne
comes out of your nose
about something so trivial
you can't remember it later –
though you're sure shoes came into it
somewhere.

And, talking of shoes, where are they?
Ah, 2:00 am is on her nightly rounds.
No-one knows *why* she steals your shoes –
they don't even fit her.
If she put them on
she'd teeter like a toddler,
tiny feet slipping with each uncertain step.
Maybe she just wants to look taller.

Huddled in the corner
3:00 am remembers, weeping,
how she danced on the tables in Europe
in a borrowed tiara
and how in Africa
her moth wings mirrored moonlight.
A teardrop splashes on her shiny shoes.

4:00 am says she's a bumblebee,
keeps you awake with the buzz
and threatens to sting if you get too close
but if you're patient,
she'll let you stroke her fuzzy costume.
Loves it when you bring her flowers –
unless they're snapdragons.
She's afraid of snapdragons,
says they ate her aunty
and two of her cousins.

White-faced
and wearing a painted-on smile
5:00 am out-grims Grimaldi.
Who knows what those baggy pants are hiding –
custard pies, buckets of water,
confetti, or a dagger
stolen from the knife thrower.
Best not to turn your back on her
even when she makes you laugh.

We don't talk about 6:00 am any more.
If you knew her, you'd understand.

7:00 am,
dominatrix in black,
takes a cold shower.
Breakfasts on fruitless muesli
with a trickle of skimmed milk,
two cups of black coffee
and a defiant cigarette.
She straightens your pictures,
rearranges your books.

But before all these
comes midnight herself.
She's complicated,
unpredictable.

Yesterday she glittered in,
all eyes and lips
and slippery satin,
electric,
ready for anything
and eager for everything.
And tonight?
Tonight she slips gentle into your bed,
sighs softly
and snuggles down.

Beauty

'I love you.' Pause. 'I *love* you.'

Fifty-five years and more she's said these words
And meant them every time.
He's always answered.
Now, though, she says them like a spell,
Words that may for a moment lift the curse
And wake her sleeping prince.

'I love you.' Breathe. 'I *love* you.'

An urgency for some response.
This is the only magic she can use.
She'd knit him shirts of nettle with blistered hands
If that would work
But he's no swan-prince, and her hands
Can only grasp and still his restless hands.

'I love you.' Wait. 'I *love* you.'

The words are weakening. One day soon
The spell will have no power to wake the sleeper.
Soon. Not today.
Eyes focus on her face, the open mouth

Forms blurred but welcome words.
'I love you.' Yes! 'I love you too.'
She bends to kiss him, for a moment
More beautiful than any fairy tale.

RICHARD C. MATHER

First Sentence

I cannot remember my first word,
but I do recall my first sentence:
cribbed in a box with the lid on,
kept under house arrest
by a familial jailer.
Sheets were hot wet prisons.

Hands larger than God
executed your angry reprisals.
I was moon-stricken, heart-bitten
by your iceberg pettiness,
and your lazy, shameful fumblings.
I could not win as you raged like some fallen idol.

Verbal bullets pierced the sweating air
when hard white fingers tore my skin
and pulled at my hair.
No night was safe from your hooks
or sour tongue.

You were the immovable statue
and your new husband a grey shadow
flat and cringing,
cowering like a frightened schoolboy
beneath the blackboard.

A litany of orders diminished us.
We sang distant tiny echoes
of your merciless overture.
You always were the one
with the chalk in your hand.

The strings snapped from your fingers,
unleashing a tentacled monster

lavishing its poison over gaunt faces.
You should have finished me
before I got you.

Like a wounded animal grasping
at its half-devoured prey
you shrank in the doorway,
hissing and spitting as I gathered up
the bags and clothes that littered the garden.
I had to escape, they tell me.
I had to escape.

My departure was almost a calling.

JOHN G. HALL

Communion

My mother brings my father's God to him
in a small leather bag every Sunday morning.
God travels the road snagged in her pocket
smuggled past betting shop & doctor's office.

He travels through streets holy incognito
freshly cooked, dreaming of tasty souls
grace wriggling amongst her shopping.
A last meal served by a mother to some
other mother's son, a-ring-a-roses of pietàs.

God undressed, a white poppy rolled in flour
is eaten unseasoned by snaked tongues, power
and glory, going, going gone! She turns the sack
inside out in case a piece of Jesus has hung back,
then tucks God's carrion bag in her top drawer along
with her sympathy cards & the comfort of crumbs.

Sing the Song of All

When the biopsy comes back
I can't help but think
where the fuck is Spiderman
when you really need him?

Where is that Buddha boy
when loneliness strangles you
and the street poets sell out
for a hand full of applause?

When the Super Ego comes dancing
beside itself with sweet reflections,
where is the Woody Guthrie man
to sing the blues to our glories?

This machine kills fascists, the prophet's guitar made its
                                   promise.
So,
where are the wire-haired highwaymen when we most need
                                   them?
Where is the match to Blake's burning bow, to the ribbon of
                                   road?

Oh yes when the gold around your soapy necks
and the discrete metals in your mobile phones
come already blood-stained from the Congo.

I can't help but think where the fuck is Tarzan
when you really need him, when black massacres
black to feed white greed for the Earth's resources?

I can't help but think where the fuck is Buddha boy
when you really need him, when Olympic China
burns the world's ozone as it floats over old Tibet?

Yeah! Where the fuck is Spiderman
when you really, really need him?

Marvin Cheeseman

Heaven Knows I'm Middle Class Now

I was happy in the gloom of a Netto store
but heaven knows I'm middle-class now

I was looking for some wine, a decent Sauvignon Blanc, and
heaven knows Netto didn't have any

In my life, why should I waste valuable time,
in supermarkets that only stock one type of hummus?

I was looking for a school to send my daughter to, that wasn't
over-run by chavs

I was looking for a school and then I found a school... and
heaven knows I had to up sticks and move to a different
catchment area

In my life, why should I give valuable time, to people who
wear nothing other than gymnasium clothing?

I used to think the rich should subsidise the less well off, but
heaven knows I'm all in favour of the abolition of inheritance
tax now

I used to get the *Mirror*, but now it's the *Daily Mail*, 'cause
heaven knows I'm a shallow, self-obsessed, uncaring, narrow-
minded, thoroughly obnoxious, totally despicable, Nazi
bastard now.

The Wholesomeness Of Coldplay and Their Fans – Lines Written at Old Trafford, Late Summer 2009

A squeaky-clean affair indeed
Not a trace of crack or weed
Coldplay fans formed ordered queues
For T-shirts, programmes, pies and booze
Prim and proper, well-behaved
Nothing vulgar or depraved
Just well-heeled well-scrubbed punters where
Not one foul word defiled the air
No low-life scum to lower the tone
Not one pint pot of piss got thrown
Not one theft, not one arrest
Cliff Richard would have been impressed
Chris Martin, arms outstretched divine
My bottled water turned to wine
This saintly chap sang one last song
The congregation sang along
Then left blessed cleansed and holier
To gently paint the town magnolia.

Rebecca Audra Smith

Hutch

He was a rabbit in bed
nibbled on my clitoris
like fresh lettuce
or carrot orange

The insidious wet
of a mouth waiting
to swallow

I could have been
a hutch shaped hole
and I don't think
he'd have noticed

I spread myself like jam
over the white bread
of the bed sheets
strawberry deep in myself
my sticky pulp taste
on my lips

The graze of his teeth on my tits
His burrow stench still mats
my hair's length

The City Fell in Love

The traffic light got a hard on
When it saw you, stayed
Permanent green
The car drivers all stopped for you to cross
Beaming their sullenness into smiles
The city fell in love with you

Tramps offered their change
For you to spend on latte and blueberry muffins
Which was free anyway as the Starbucks
Boy holds you, dream girl, in his arms
You and your happiness and your hickies
Your neck a bitten mess
Its red flaring against a shirt's collar
You, and your permanent zebra crossings
Your zigzag from pavement to pavement
You are a blaring stop sign.

BEN MELLOR

S&M Food

This isn't just food,
This is sex
Dressed as a chef's
Wet dream and served
To you with lashings
Of creamy velvet voiceover,
Seductively hinting at
The intimate moments
Of indulgence to be discovered
Beneath the revealing layers
Of soft-focus sensual imagery
Depicting dribbling juices,
And quivering fleshy forms,
Titillating and tantalising
Your salivating taste buds,
This is high class
Gastronomic porn.

This isn't soul food
This is stick-it-in-your-hole-food,
This isn't cold food
This is so-fucking-hot food,
This is take a little taste
And then plunge
Into the pot food,
This isn't polite food,
This isn't nice food,
This is adulterated
Vice food,
This is rude.
This is S&M Food.

This isn't just nature's booty
This is yummy mummy Earth herself,
Fresh from the fields and feeling
Rather fruity, buxom, bountiful,
Ample and juicy,
This isn't just some two-bit
Cheap and nasty floozy,
Some bargain basement basics
No frills value
Can of cat food
This is a divine
Diva of delights,
This is one of
Botticelli's nudes,
Laced-up in push-ups
And suspenders to whet
Your appetite and get you
In the mood,
Frisky and feisty
And ready to be subdued.
She's giving you full permission
To play with your food.

This isn't cheap,
Sweet and sour,
Pay-by-the hour food,
This is five-star hotels
And champagne in the shower food,
This is trussed-up, glistening
And ready to devour food,
This isn't 0 to tasty in 90 seconds
This is savour the flavour all night
And feel in power food
This is our food
This is S&M Food.

And while you're glued
By your own juices to
The Cordon Bleu movies
We create to seduce you
Pay no attention to rumours
You may have heard of abuses,
Our food's Fair Trade,
Seasonal, and organically reared,
These cash-cows willingly surrendered
Their rumps to be seared,
They virtually volunteered for this bondage,
We've been in this business for years
And not a single one has absconded,
Our food wants to be wanted,
It wants you to possess it,
Don't you see those eyes behind the veil
Just begging you to undress it,
It wants to be spread like a whore's legs
On your plate and liberated
Through being digested
Like Palestinians living on contested territory
Who eventually will reap the benefits
Of our prosperity.
(The analogy might be crude
But we're sure you can see the truth)
So just hold your head still and don't move,
While we shower you in money shots
That can be swallowed
Without being chewed,
This is lewd,
This is S&M Food.

IAN HOWELLS

Back Piccadilly

There are old men whose faces are reddened by booze,
Playing a game that they're destined to lose,
Living a lifestyle that no one would choose,
On the streets round the station near midnight

Where the girls from the East sell themselves on the street,
Flogging their bodies like pieces of meat,
They'll fuck, wank and suck on a semen-stained sheet,
On the streets round the station near midnight

Near the broken-down warehouse with chains on the doors,
There are young men who fight as they eye up the whores,
Their blood wets the pavement as they settle scores,
On the streets round the station near midnight,

In a phone box a girl who might once have had charm,
Stares into my eyes with a look of alarm,
Then relaxes and fixes a spike in her arm,
On the streets round the station near midnight

I look out of my window through sunshine and glare,
At the guy on the steps with the White Lightning stare,
And the comforting bottle, and I know he'll be there,
As the hour hand ticks back round to midnight

STUART A. PATERSON

Unquiet Slumbers for the Sleepers

*"... and wondered how any one could ever imagine unquiet
slumbers for the sleepers in that quiet earth."
– (Emily Brontë, Wuthering Heights)*

Night vibrates to the far-near saw & hum
of motorway & airport, now & then
gets gutted by high otherworldly screams
wrenched out of helpless animals
or those we dare not think about
for fear they might be out there.

Mostly, though, this place limps past
on crippling clocks, a creaking door,
low-volume late-night TV shows, a lonely
child's baby snores along the corridor,
the whispering nib occasional on forms
defining lives, routines, ourselves.

In daytime, chaos kicks you from behind
or chucks a cup or sets off fire alarms
& runs away while telling you to go & fuck
yourself. At night, it sleeps the way that
children should, wrapped tight in cartoon
duvet covers, cotton wool & splayed
like spiders, limbs akimbo on soft beds
in rooms knee-deep in vital clutter.

Silence, here, is bought by tiredness
of every kind, not word or plastic panacea,
& through it, every night, I walk afraid
of waking them before the crashing
sound of one more day that really breaks.

GORDON ZOLA

That's Me

I go by the name of Gordon Zola
I'm more champagne than Coca Cola.
More Cooper Clark than Andrew Motion.
More River Irwell than Atlantic Ocean.

But...

I'm easily seduced by any love potion.
Coz that's me.

More Robin Hood than William Tell.
More Leonard Cohen than Soft Cell.
I've seen both heaven and the fires of hell.

But... that's me.

More Cheddar cheese than coq au vin
More off the cuff than cunning plan.
I'm as randy as a rutting ram.

Coz that's me.

I'm the sum of my parts and much more.
And if you get real close I might open the door
And let you see that sometimes I'm unsure.
I sometimes ding when I should dong.
I often sing when I don't know the song.
I strive to do right but sometimes do wrong.

Coz that's me.

I'm more Ark of the Covenant than Noah's Ark.
More Ryan Giggs than Ji-Sung Park.
My bite's sometimes worse than my bark.
Coz that's me.

More complex than the offside rule.
I'm deeper than the deepest pool.
But at the end of the day, I'm nobody's fool
Coz that's me.

More D'Artagnan than Cardinal Richelieu.
I'm softer than a Kleenex tissue.
But I prefer a Big Mac to a *Big Issue*.

Coz that's me.

I'm a Gemini with a Libran moon.
On the odd occasion I've come too soon.
But I'm more court jester than buffoon.

Coz that's me.

I can be colder than an Arctic winter.
My mind runs faster than an Olympic sprinter.
I'm more puzzling than a play by Pinter.

Coz that's me.

More Patrick Stewart than Patrick Swayze.
More Dalai Lama than Ian Paisley.
But I have been known to drive you fucking crazy.

Coz that's me.

Definitely more Spike Milligan than Spike Lee.
More Cappuccino coffee than cup of tea.
And if you get real close I might let you see me as I really am.
Just like you I'm doing the best that I can.
My life's a litany of ecstasy and error.
My day's littered with both joy and terror.

But I'll never give up till the bitter end.
Coz life's not that bitter. I'll just smile and titter.

Coz that's me… And I make no apology.

Cheez

Cheez: lovely chunks of cheez.
Beats magic mushrooms, acid or Es
It's better than sex, it'll blow your mind.
And unlike masturbation, you'll never go blind.

I had a girl friend, alas I lost her. She said
'I draw the line at Double Gloucester'.
She used to talk dirty about Gouda.
'Louder', I cried as I fed her
I love the way her lips caressed
my chunk of Cheddar. But she gave me
the sack, did a runner with Monterey Jack.

Cheez: lovely chunks of cheez.

If you do Parmesan, I'm your man.
I go silly for Caerphilly, off my tree for Brie
and nothing can compare to Camembert.
I could kill for Red Leicester and have to
confess to bending more forks than Uri Geller
bingeing on Mozzarella in the cellar.

Cheez: lovely chunks of cheez.
Beats magic mushrooms, acid or Es
It's better than sex, it'll blow your mind.
And unlike masturbation, you'll never go blind.

I once went on a spree with Dairylea.
I used to love it wrapped until I got trapped
in an eternal triangle with Primula and Kraft.
It was only Mascarpone that stopped me feeling lonely.

Cheez: lovely chunks of cheez.

I now need a fix of cheese sticks
to feed my habit of Welsh rarebit.
I crave cheese with everything, even
spam, you may think me a sad man.

But in the words of Rhet Buttler
from *Gone With the Wind*
'Frankly, I don't give Edam'

Cheez, lovely chunks of cheez.
Beats magic mushrooms, acid or Es
It's better than sex, it'll blow your mind.
And unlike masturbation, you'll never go blind.

Cheez, lovely chunks of cheez.

To the tune of 'Turning Japanese' by The Vapors

I think I'm turning into cheez.
I think I'm turning into cheez.
I think I'm turning into cheez.
I really think so.

BRINK

Basket Weaving

You cut off your mother's face
and stitched it onto the cat?

I shuffle feet and pull a George Doubya face.
It is too cold in here and I want to shroud myself
in tight arms, but know this is a game of
body language: I have already moved my chair
so that you are not a silhouette. Now
I wonder how you view yourself;
whether you really exist or are just the end
product of compulsory training courses,
laced-up and wiped-down like some token gesture
I'd recommend you keep the receipt for.
Your tedious rote will be cheaper
when the paperback comes out.
I hear its pages turn as you uncross your legs
and sigh whilst my thoughts manage to get lost
in a cul-de-sac.

My smile is encouraging.
Time and sun have moved on and back to square one,
I am squinting like a lab technician with a hangover.
If I could see your expression
I probably wouldn't care.
I rub sleep from an eye and try
to recall the day I got old:
my skin feels loose and puffy and I
want to help you with your homework.

I'm going to recommend
we try you on a new course.

Your certificates claim that you
have completed them.

Unnatural Practices of Country Folk

Berate a badger,
Cup a squirrel's nads,
Poke an owl and
Slap a stoat:
For these be the ways of country folk.

Goat punchers and geese goosers
Who are more than happy to
Fondle an unsuspecting duck
Tickle a cow or
Nudge a pony
When they want to push their luck.

Such quaint ways –
But it's tradition, they say.
Like hunting foxes for fun and
Shooting at things
With a fucking great gun.

But, that's what you get
When your sister's your mum.

JOHN SIDDIQUE

Desire for Sight (After Lorca)

When gossip starts all that is left is gossip.
When fear takes hold, all that is left is the fear.
Fold away your papers,
colour in the outlines.
Regret is the first town our train will pass though.
Unknowing, the confusion of unknowing.
Let my country see itself,
may its people be visible to each other.

To the Iron Waters

From our house at Regent Street,
out from the family firing line,
by passing each netted window,
a street full of Catholics.
The red phone box by the junkyard
in the distance, a first marker.
Then the anarchist A in a circle
sprayed onto the wall one night in 1977
in a hopeful pink enamel.

Folly Walk where I sometimes speak
to the tramp who makes the bench there
his morning checkpoint,
Red Stripe in his hand.
'It settles the nerves,' he says.

Opening out,
Cronkeyshaw Common.
The bus stop at Syke Common where
we hang in the evening, each one of us
is in love with Anna Duffy, she only
goes out with lads with cars.

Into the green,
tracking the pubs,
The Donkey, The Hunter's Rest.
A private fishing lodge where Kevin Isaac
shot birds, and I cried at their small limpness.

To the Iron Waters,
freezing over red stones.
A mouthful for a tonic. Bathing
your feet for waking up and forgetting.

HELÊN THOMAS

On Being a White Square

I'm a crisp linen table cloth lovingly laundered,
A communion wafer that's strangely four cornered,
I'm a canvas primed for a colourful brush,
Or a fresh fall of snow before treading to slush,
For industrious Inuit I am a brick,
I'm a glue-crafting child's chiselled Pritt Stick,
I'm a slippery, hard slab of heart stopping lard,
Or a mini hotel fridge cooling the bar,
I'm a wedding cake, frosted, its details awaiting,
I'm a Christmas card ice-rink ready for skating,
Perhaps I'm a sugar lump plopped into tea,
Or an empty price tag on something that's free,
I'm a synthetic moon for mass manufacture,
A monologue script improvised by an actor,
I'm a homemade cube of peppermint cream,
The record of last night's unrecalled dream,
I'm next year's photograph album's first page,
I'm an old lady's age.
I'm a gallon of milk in a transparent tank,
An ungrateful person's letter of thanks,
I'm a naked calendar lacking a date,
I'm the nouvelle cuisine emperor's new plate,
I'm an anorexic's favourite menu,
The last man on Earth's party venue,
A four walled tunnel's end that's in sight,
Might be, maybe, a square of light.

SIMON RENNIE

Marmalade

Life taken takes life from those left living,
At least for a while. She could sail no more
Between doldrums and the swirling maelstrom
Of violent grief – the gift that keeps giving,
The loss that leaves her lost at sea before
Stranded on shores there is no escape from.
Every object, every everyday chore
Serves as a reminder of her loved one;
He is gone. He is still here. He is gone.
He pervades each room from ceiling to floor.

And the great healer plays its dirty tricks
Brings days of numbness that disguise the pain
Before, voila! – the curtain is lifted,
Reveals the dodgy shelf he did not fix,
The garden shoes hardened by summer rain,
The mess by the stairs he never shifted;
Banality bites over and again.
Barely noticed before, necessity
Exposes its god-awful drudgery;
Its solemn dirge and incessant refrain.

But despite setbacks distance is some shield
And what they all say turns out to be true;
The act of living means new life is made
And small joys appear that once were concealed.
Almost enough to believe she'll come through
When after weeks she finds the marmalade.
It happens again – all the grief comes anew;
This half-jar, his favourite with thick shreds,
How they'd lived life inside each other's heads.
I love you. I did love you. I love you.

Listening at the Statue to the Fallen

Do you remember how the bronze bouquet
  Would sway in the wind on Angel Hill?
Those blue-green leaves against the grey
  Skies are held aloft to this day still –
Though never still – the city's thrum
  Plays a chord on them for its own ear
Enticing those alive to come
  Embrace the dead remembered here.

And here our grass-stained jeans would kneel,
  Our bark-rough hands would press the stone.
    Braving the wind we would hear the words
Sung aloud for all who feel
  Or ever felt – you are not alone
    We wished or thought we heard.

JENNIE B

Leaves

Back then I loved to watch the bees
buzzing in lavender; I felt I was there again,
and when I remember you, I think of trees.

The sky was bluer than all the seas;
I gazed upward avoiding the yellow flame.
Back then I loved to watch the bees.

I climbed a sycamore, felt the soft breeze
carry the smell of growth: the green spring rain,
and when I remember you, I think of trees.

I tried to hide behind the star-shaped leaves,
willed them to fall in short-lived fame.
Back then I loved to watch the bees.

On that wooden floor, I wished time would freeze:
like us, branches entwined, became the same,
and when I remember you, I think of trees.

I kissed you and you tasted of memories.
Bitter-tainted. Never to happen again.
Back then I loved to watch the bees
and when I remember you, I think of trees.

Qing Ming Festival

Alone, on the eve of Qing Ming,
In my Cheetham Hill flat
I light three joss sticks
In a willow-patterned rice bowl
Full of sand; put on a tape
Of Huangmei opera
From my hometown.

A tattered copy of Du Mu's poetry
– *Qing Ming Si Jie Yu Fei Fei*...
Lies next to a plate of fried noodles
Like Grandma used to make.
Offering it to her in my mother's tone
I then eat it myself with relish
As in my hunger-perforated childhood.

The paper money bought from Chinatown
Grows in glamour as I gaze at the gilded edge
– too luxurious for the Grandma I knew;
She would refuse to use the notes
As she did with everything good; they were
Always pressed into my hand, so
Why wait for her to hand them back?

I shall exchange them for an incense burner
For the next Qing Ming festival
So the joss sticks won't fall
And my prayers will rise with the smoke
The cloud of my loneliness
Telling her the aching feeling
I have for home.

Homage to Baba

My memories, like feeding fish, intermittently surface.
The focus, always Baba's sallow-skinned gaunt face.
No open wounds or abscess, but invisible sores
Bleeding away his spirit and physical strength
Amid the wonders in my then-childly eyes –
Delicate needles twirling in the doctor's plump hands,
Bamboo sucking-cups drawing purple rings
On his back, where the doctor's deft hands knead.
I watched wide-eyed, spellbound, yet unable to ignore
The bitter odour of root-herbs boiling on the mud stove
And the fear of something unseen eating my Baba away.

RACHAEL K

Crow's Transition

Eventually
Crow came out.
Fight-talking.
Out from the mouthy-hole of a dark green wilderness
into the face-to-face
the gaping gawk water.

A squawking puddle of mud light.

Crow looked down.
'Wait. Stop. Please stop. No!'
Too late.
There it was.
Their eyes met.
Everything bothersome appeared
to be his
welcomed him
and did the splits
jazz-handedly in spandex
and ballet shoes
laughtering
hysterically pointedly
with bells on.
"Toppermost twigger!"
"Leaf wigger!"

He couldn't shake it off.
Crow felt blacker and redder and greener than ever.

'Say Queer,' said God with her tongue among his cheeks
'Say Queer,' said God playfully with her bite around his neck
'Say Queer!'

Her knowing was moving inside him.
Fuck. God. Mother. Why?
Retching realisations.

The world started quivering in a booming falsetto
Crow heard it viscerally
It touched him
wrongly
with unbearable slowness
he began
learning-into-being
mirroring
parrot fashion.

On the other hand,
If it rained now he would be free.
But if he was free a song might fill his heart!
And then what?

'Look at me!' he pecked

'Look at me, dejected !'

'Look at me!'
'Look at me!'
'Look at me!'
'Look at me!'
'Look at me!'
'Look at me!'

'I'm beautiful!'

... meanwhile;
above the faux despairing morning and
the skinning screams and the squeamishness
– but below the clamouring parliament of the upper
guttering –

Budgie smiled down,
(giggled even?)

and swallowed
and pursed.

She tweeted once or twice,
for her gathering
and went back to noticing her cage.

ROGER NICHOLS

First Flight

To have grasped the full measure
and scope of where I lived
was a fact, not an obvious pleasure.

I knew at garden height
where this lay in relation to that,
but had no idea that a flight

in a plane would
make a wood plain
or plainer.

But the sight of all that
from unusual height
held the world I had built
about myself up to a mirror
made of distorting tin-foil,

and for a long time afterwards
I would look at the soil
in the garden. My mind flew

outward in all directions,
trying to reassemble
what I had seen from there,
at a tilt.

DARREN THOMAS

Larry the Lobster

Larry the Lobster boarded a train
and made his way to London Euston
but he didn't have a ticket
and so the guard threw him off,
ironically, at Crewe Station.

Benny-Jo Zahl

Swagger

Now then.
Let's get a few
things straight.

I know at first glance
I'm little more
than a thug,
a Salford boy's swagger,
close cropped hair
on my head.

I love little more
than cuddles in bed.

A bottle of whiskey
some fat rock-star lines
and some flat-lining green.
I long to have the strength
of the teetotaller in my dreams
but I'm surrounded by dealers
wasters and thieves.

You know you're in the wrong place
when the whole room laughs
as a sted 'ed recounts
the taking of life.
    "I know it looks bad,"
he says with a smile
        "but at the time
        I didn't know she
        was carrying child."

School-yard bullies
playing merciless games
  "*Hide the blade in the rib cage,*"
Just for looking this way I escaped.

But most didn't.

I left them behind.

Brothers, lovers,
friends of mine.
And I'll remember them all
'till I'm old and haggard.
'cos there's so much
you can't read,
from a Salford boy's swagger

MARK FORSHAW

Proposal

Such scenes do not take place
under these conditions.
We dream of something other
than the silent excretions of mice
and canopies of frozen breath
hanging above a spongy bed.

Where now we have the darkness
and, despite the cold,
the damp compression of arms and legs,
we should have luxuries instead:
warmth and food and wine, or tissues
to mop your tears and clumsy phrases.

But this night has no design,
no frills to dull the doubt,
the gnawing doubt, I have always felt.
Something old crawls from out of my mouth
and moves across your shaking face
whose blind wetness I hold in the dark.

JULIA DEAKIN

Winfield Ruled

Between WE ARE CLOSING and WE ARE CLOSED
we press cold noses to the glass, sniffing at the past.
This paper white-out draws us in a way that lately
double doors and all that red and white busyness did not.

Inside stands a four year-old with sixpence among trays
of cut-throat Christmas baubles, notepads and Tiny Tears.
Down the street she's not keeping up with Dad's answer
to *how can such big blocks of chocolate be so cheap?*

There's my grammar-school friend Frances enthroned
at her Saturday job till in Piccadilly Gardens, *Europe's largest
Woolworths*, saying she'll leave us soon to work there full time.
There! By the steps where half Manchester first kissed –

and where later *Evening News* photographers caught limbs
flailing between smoke and window grills.
Foam-filled furniture, pre-sprinkler valves, the killer.
Ten people and an era dead.

Then me again, queuing with my last ever Woolies purchase
and – as lavatory brushes aren't things you hold for long –
smalltalking with the next woman, also buying one.
Great minds think alike the opener, no doubt.

We stood about where on the lanes of dull wood laminate
those dusty racks now wait between a pair of captive staff,
one phoning someone, while behind her two Coca-Cola logos
tangle over bare chiller cabinets, like graveyard worms.

PAM LEESON

Dancer

I watch her move through the world
as though it were kind

land on it with a smile
it doesn't deserve

arm stretched for a first wish

winding the air and leaving it sweet.
innocent still
even though she doesn't know

at a glimpse of my girl
I'm left glad and sad
and wondering about salvation

one day I know that I will look
and not know

one day the world will take her

one day I will look
and not recognise my daughter

SHIRLEY NICHOLSON

Reconciled

He sent an emu's egg, carefully wrapped,
with coral from the Great Barrier Reef,
a kangaroo fur bag, two oyster shells
he'd brought up from the ocean's depth
which she treasured, fingered, arranged,
then rearranged with the greatest care.
And whenever she found a wishing well
she threw in a coin, wished like prayer.

He came back, but it was years later
when there was scarcely a hope left in her
and those wishing wells held no more charm.
Then one night he came to her with a book,
'We were two horses, your mother and I,
who tossed their manes, pulled different ways.'
He opened the book, knelt by her bed
and softly read her a poem he loved.

JUSTIN WALSH

Dog on a String

Let's play this tape forward, through showers of silver light,
Spider dreaming, stolen giros, swimming-born horses.
Spools of dark passageways and ghosts of Christmas past.
On pigeon wings, flightless, broken.
The stumbled future now privy,
Hobbling, bleary, dog shit drizzled, city centre archways.
Reel of Princess Parkway.
Grey floors, walls, ceiling, sky.
Forgotten linen flaps on pubic washing line.
Chains flush, tourniquet blooms beneath lamp lights.
Casting no shadow, no reflection. Jostle over this dimp, that
                                                    scrap.
Foaming-mouthed refuges bicker in the pavement gloom.
Guttersnipe poltergeists, dressed to kill.
Me, an Armageddon Fagin, you, 'the Artful Dodger'.
'Rent and gent,' she called us that,
When there was room, still, for us to laugh.
Four arms, legs, two heads, the other half to the puzzle
Pouring the lodger's cup into each other.
We share T-shirts, trainers, undies 'n' works.
Living in your pocket, you in mine.
Slipping endlessly through the holes, the cracks.
The crack.
Bruised arms an Ordnance Survey map
Of this time and that, adventures once had.
Like John and Yoko, bed-ins for days.
We never kiss though, never spoon. Back to back, you and me.
'Spoons are only good for cooking up.' You smile when you say
                                                    it.
I scream into my pillow, I think that you know.
'I can't,' you still say, 'I just can't'.
Pushing me away to that place in your past.

Scene fades into white noise of traffic.
Trumpets chorus for *Coronation Street* adverts
And teddy bears' picnic ice-cream van.
White blood freezes like the first rust of cocaine
When you once held me at arm's length,
Eyes thick with autumn tears as yet uncried
That trickled leaves and formed ship canals of
Pink clean pink satin.
Beneath the dirt and grime of another night
I wait, I pray for all of this to end.
And toast mayflies, toast mayflies.

MATTHEW CURRY

And the Palm Trees Whose Leaves Are Fraying

And the palm trees whose leaves are fraying,
and whose trunks are trussed up with string, seem to be saying:
nothing, nothing at all's decaying.

The dolphin fountain sends up its spout,
and the children sitting in their buggies gasp and shout,
and the glass, the glass in the dome wants out.

Pink marble, a popcorn smell, brass rails,
the galleries of shops getting ready for the sales,
and the night, the night in here just pales.

Pastel portraits in a realist mode,
the dome and the Roman columns dredge a code:
what you'll get, what you'll get, and what's owed.

And the palm trees whose leaves are fraying,
and whose trunks are trussed up with string, seem to be saying:
nothing, nothing at all's decaying.

CHERYL PEARSON

Sometime Before Dawn

Pre-dawn I wake, and your breathing finds me,
places me in this bed, this room, this
sudden not-quite-morning. You won't mind me
folding into your side, so I fold; kiss

the tangled mat of hair on your bent arm;
smell the yeasty smell which makes your skin taste
of wheat. Once, in Wales, we went to a farm
where a similar smell rose from the waste

of horses – a homely smell, redolent
of good earth, heat, sweat, physical labour.
I tucked myself into you, nonchalant.
Breathed you in as I do now, bed-neighbour

on this dark dawn, as the clock enforces
order and you dream – perhaps of horses.

Penelope

Dignified, you weave your decadent shroud,
embroidering each stitch with queenly calm.
You will not be touched; each new Prince or King
is warned. *Leave her be. You must let her grieve.*
first. Let her finish weaving. Let her thread
spell out her sadness – ring her hand with gold

after. You know full well they want your gold,
your breasts in either hand, your crown. The shroud,
if all goes well, will best their greed; the thread
you stitch so tight by day unpicked by calm,
determined hands each night. And so you grieve,
grieve, braiding out your sorrow for the King

your heart is slyly sure still lives, the King
ingested years ago by the warm, gold
mouth of the horizon. How long you grieve
in peace depends on your performance: shroud
your cunning, keep your head, think only calm
thoughts. Steady any trembles with your thread.

You keep a little of each scene you thread
to hush the queries you pre-empt: *the King
has been gone how long? Still she sews?* Bent, calm
at your work, the patterns gild your knee, gold
lattice, lace, gilt tapestry – all shroud
the anxious tapping of your feet. You'd grieve

for years, but fear you lack the nerve to grieve
forever. They drink your husband's wine, thread
his gems at their throats, claim the beds and shroud
their shoulders in his furs. *When I am King –*
you hear their boasts and dream of murder. Gold
blade through the breast. Death in short order. Calm

in the palace... No. Breathe. Will yourself calm.
Your husband will return, and they will grieve
each slur, each smutty look, each joke. The gold
band of your wedding ring gleams as you thread.
Turned to pig by witch, ash by death... no King
of yours would go so readily. The shroud

unfolds in your calm, capable hands. Thread
picked. Stitched. Picked. Stitched. *I will not grieve. My King
is not dead.* Gold eyes fixed fast on the shroud.

Pulling Through

He watches the ward clock, auditing
her slow breath: she has gone where
he cannot reach her. A flock of waders
bothering the shoreline of her sleep
fades into the soothe of warm waves
falling. Currents lift her all night,
adrift under unfamiliar stars, the hug
of darkness, a hurtling moon.

Now the tide turns. In new light
she is cast up through breakers
onto the bleak beach where he,
eyes aching from vacancy,
waits for her face to turn
towards him, to smile.

December City

Whiffs of glühwein sharpen the drizzle,
couples stay close in shadow-thick squares.
I push softly into the margins
through soap-hearts, strangers, a posse of trees;
the past unspools in onions, carols,
a smattering of stars.

LINDA COSGRIFF

Find a Solution

Infants once played in this
ruptured field.
Now, each night is Kristallnacht,
bottles broken over
foreign heads.
Adolescents scorn childhood friends,
despise them like yellow stars
on skeleton men in
some other Holocaust.
Stolen cars churn dried
blood and grass
like Nazi ash.
In overlooking houses,
faces turn to
safer sights and latent
Adolfs beat their wives;
pride in their little Reichs.

ANGELA TOPPING

Nights in the Old City

There's something dying in this place tonight.
It wrestles with the dark but cannot last.
The streets are wet and comfortless. Neon
lights flicker, blue and red like glittering fish,
incongruous against the ancient stones.

There's plenty of time for talking as we sit,
coffee cooling past its power to soothe.
Your naked glance, despairing, catches me
off guard; I am unable to perform
my usual magic trick of raising smiles.

You measure time in cigarettes while I
sip cognac, try to thaw your mood.
We risk a walk despite the rain and find
a draughty church; with votive candles lit,
we watch the shadows flutter crazily,
talk of old inevitable things.

FRANCESCA PRIDHAM

Accident

The gasman calls. Blood on my T-shirt
startles him. 'What's happening here?' he says.
I can't speak, my son hiding in the front room,
we need the cooker in the kitchen and my baby's blood
won't stop spreading through my clothes.

'Her finger's come off,' I say;
holding it in place, a blood stained flannel
slips as I speak. 'Matt,' I try to shout;
how can I be angry with a boy
shocked into a tight ball?

The split in my head is great. 'Matt,' I call.
Emily cross-legged in her school hall
would have found my bag. 'Matt,' gently now,
'I need your help.' The gasman reaches for the phone.

When we return, I have Matt by the hand
though his eyes will not look at me.
Hannah's hand bandaged, she sleeps.

I see the gasman's put the cooker in,
left things out for a cup of tea.

DAVE RIGBY

My World is Five Foot Eight

with bright black obsidian eyes
and painted hair, her heart
pinned to her T-shirt sleeve hidden
beneath a shop full of overcoats
she dreams
thoughts thick as treacle
yet pure as the finger nails of a newborn.
I give thanks and look over my shoulder
as the grocer weighs out my emotions
on dubious scales.
we gaze at the swings
but somehow end up whirling round.
as my grip slips
I wonder if there's enough woodchip in the world.
she has all the elegance of a sewing pattern
too complex for a novice like me.
a fist full of thimbles yet
still the needle connects. prick. I am six foot four but
                              from a distance smaller.

MANTZ YORKE

The Boat

Out of the grizzly sea's immediate reach
the boat seems disproportionate
against the harbour wall, as if too gross
for the tiny port. Stretched overthin,
the tide – mere puddles on the shaly flat –
lets me crunch a track across mussel-beds
and snails towards the silhouettes collecting,
insect-like, around its bulk. Closer to,
the hull, dully striped along its planks
in blue, white and red, shows distant foam
beneath the concave keel, and a cooker lies
face-down on blackish wrack: only now I see
scattered on this placid-looking shore
the unshattered screen, mechanic's oil-can
and splintered piece of mast, and understand

the random strew of plastic film I'd seen
between the nabs. Folk compose their smiles
before this hulk, ignoring the excited kids
scrabbling among the ruptured bilges'
miscellany of crabs and headless fish, the sketcher
on his folding chair, and the dog scampering,
claw in mouth, about their legs. Standing off,
my zoom lens frames a photograph: the wreck
whose blood surrounds an archipelago of weed,
and lacy waves rearing up and toppling
on a hidden reef. Beyond crumbling cliffs
a fisherman is trundling salvage to the quay:
as I catch him and his barrowload of bits
he glances towards my camera, and spits.

KESS TAMBLYN

Persephone

'You'll have to leave sometime,'
he murmurs into the fossil of your spine,
soft divine scatterings littering your cosy burrow home
in the soft lime light from above,
his pebble fingers tracing the bow of your lips,
as you close blissful eyes
and curl into his devil shape.
'Not yet,' you whisper in return, 'it's too late,
now, to go back.'

'They'll be waiting,'
he nudges you, later,
as you lie in tender arms,
smiling in the dying shadow of Mephistopheles' charms.
No alarm bells – there are no sirens
here. 'It'll do no harm,' you shake your head
ruefully, 'to stay here for a while.'
'How long?' He cannot hide the hope.
The jagged slope leading up, back,
home, is somehow sprinkled with fear. 'Say...
a year?'

'Really?'
Suddenly he is all energy,
boundless hope, excitement, joy.
Sweet boy. 'Really,' you promise,
a smile in your eyes. He believes your lies.
Because, really, how can you stay?
This is bliss, this personal hell,
this grey area, where daylight
is green from the grass above your head

and you live your own way
among the vivacity of the dead.
But it can't last.

You are the sensible one,
the practical, think-things-through, serious one,
but as time goes on
and he loves you more and more and more,
as you come to see happiness, always, as green,
as darkness, to you, dances that thin line
between routine and new,
as you become at home in grey,
begin to dread the day,
begin to pray – not for salvation,
but for security – you can't help yourself.
You begin to wonder

what if?
And one day, when his adoring fingers
are plaiting with lovely doting care
your maiden's hair, and his lips are sighing
kisses on your heart, you crack.
Of course you can't leave. Of course you can't.
Because…

you love him.

That's all it takes.
Suddenly, you're on your feet: anxious,
desperate now. You're incomplete
alone, but with him…
somehow, he makes you, you.
He's panicking, wondering what's wrong.
You're frantic, needy, happy.
You'll work it out,
somehow you'll stay. You'll find a way,
even if it kills you.

And you do.
The forbidden fruit –
as old as time itself, or at least as old as woman.
Pouring through books you find a clause:
she who eats of Hades' fruit,
that's it, the loot, the golden treasure –
all you have to do is
pluck
and you're his.

One. Two. Three. Four.
More. You need more.
But before your definite tender hands
can touch that fifth seed to your lips,
the gates of your own personal hell
are flung wide, you see the sky, cringe away.
The green light of day is swallowed up
in a deathly breath of fresh air,
that rugged slope thrown into light,
hell opened up
and you're dragged back up into the mortal world.
Painful eyes open to reveal your mother,
desperate, caring, best interests at heart
in a haven of sickly green living mockery.
You close them, tight, only to find him
burnt like a sepia negative into the open wound of your soul
and eight final pomegranate seeds
lying in his lifeless hands
like pebbles on the graves of the dead.

MARTIN ZARROP

Bad Day at the Office

The story changes. I know that now.
Tears become rhythm, metre, line,
a foreign language spoken by mutes
decoding ciphers in windowless cells.

Me, I keep well away from words,
look for you in stagnant pools,
lift ill-formed pebbles to your eyes;
remind myself that poets lie.

MICHAEL WILSON

Knight's Move Thinking

The weirdest little thoughts bulk up the littlest hours
Keeps your mind going laps round the living room
Spending the adverts thinking of those you've loved and left
Time on a string
The night an ever-decreasing loop of repeated programmes
The bed in the next room whispers sweet nothings through the
                                                          wall

Clockwatching the other way around
Sparking the blue touch paper of a boredom
Threaded through with dope

The strangest little revelations only come out at night
Forgotten in the blink of a channel
That life is not a vocation
For many of us it's a potting-shed hobby
And across this imagined community
There are people in the same pubs across the same cities and
                                                          towns
The same songs playing from the same jukeboxes and sound
                                                          systems
The same songs crooning softly from the same bedrooms
The same families sharing the same TV scene

And in Manchester the city is strangled by its own legacy
Buildings of now and then stand knock-kneed cheek by jowl
Working on your knees high up in a glass tower
On a task that requires all the literacy skills of a five year old
Clockwatching, time as taut as a piano wire
Always five minutes since your last fag break
Always five minutes since the clock last changed
Thinking about how earlier it felt like you fell out of bed
And landed slap bang face first on your desk

And a walk through the streets is landmarked by an A to Z of a
hundred memories
But if you stick around long enough the bitter ones get
swallowed up by the sweet
And the week runs on a maddening loop
And the months stumble into each other
And the years pick up speed
And before you know it you're staring down the wrong end of
your youth
With no way back again
Life begins every day, the world exactly as you left it
Still 17 in heart mind and soul if not body, at breakfast
wondering what Mr Kellogg's did with your toy

And trying to work out how far along you are in life
Is like staring at a giant map without a YOU ARE HERE
Nothing in your head from all those years in school
Except that Pythagoras rhyme, Venn diagrams and oxbow
lakes
Following the clockwork lifeline timetable like an on off switch
With all the wit and wisdom of knight move thinking, A to B
to C to G
Always at the height of fashion a season behind cause you shop
at TK Maxx
With a record collection that pretty much stunted and stayed
in the last 90s
Ducking questions of kids at Christmas from the elderly
relative that skipped the sherry and went straight onto the gin

And at the end of every daily odyssey you find yourself in the
same room
With the same thoughts circling above the bed enveloped in
smoke
Waiting for the bed to begin to sink under your dead weight
Waiting for the nightly surreal picture show to start
Giving in to the splendour of losing the game
And the months that shuffled past

And when gravity finally wraps itself around your body
And these words finally fade to black
Your soul will rest safe in a box stored underneath your bed

MICHELLE PARAMANANTHAM

Thoughts Such as These

It's in the way the sea almost definitely falls away at the shore,
                            she says, and kind of like
the butterflies and beetles that move through slow summers.

He likes to think it was some other kind of another thing,
                            something more like spring or
blue, perhaps, and he sticks to thoughts like these.

Together, we sit with open windows, and the smell on the
                            wind is of honey and pepper,
but nobody mentions it or wonders how it ever came about.

The birds that soar past our heads later in the day feel like the
                            idea of smaller things we
don't admit to. Things such as these puzzle us and we half
                            decide to watch the clouds
move in the changing light.

Then, slowly comes in another smell, like something bruised,
                            like something squeezed,
but nobody mentions it.

She says she sometimes gets a sense of eggs and a certain kind
                            of green but she ignores it
and wishes she never really had. These moments are too
                            plump, too quick, too past.

She knows the miniature things she could have held in both
                            hands, like a type of small
bird, but it's thoughts like these that she forgets to mention.

Two halves of nothing is almost better than a fuller something
                            else, he starts to say,

but nobody will listen and he decides to keep these bigger
thoughts for other days.

We are never almost sure if we are ever nearly living, and often
wonder if we were never nearly there.

There are many thoughts such as these that pass like leaves,
she says, he knows, we think, but nobody will admit to them.

We watch as she sort of gets up to leave and kind of then stays.
She feels she must write a letter home, and spends a day
deciding what to say.

SARAH COLLINS

From the Train

After the wood engraving by Christine Johnson, 1979

The window frames an open page
where I trace outlines of trees, some filigree,
with outer fronds that float like seaweed in watery air.
My pen follows the curved meniscus of hill,
smudges its blackness into thick white paper.
I listen for sounds that fall in step,
watch the hill drop in folds,
creased with crossings-out.
Like sheep paths among grass,
or my own, crumpled drafts.

I build a new phrase from three houses,
each word picked out in fascia of darker or lighter grey
and painted edges of brick, one door ajar,
a matchstick fence that pins them to the slope of field,
then drops to a meadow, cloistered with trees
gathered in twos and threes. Their branches spill
a pool of purple ink around their roots,
where the sun glitters a line of grass.

These trees suggest a stanza's shape,
I bend their twigs to fit each new line's break.
A cloud of doves, in flight, tilts my pen south.
Close up, the long grass cascades into ferny meadowsweet,
dark round heads of foxtail.
My pen lands against a tangled nest.
I push out some boundaries,
draw others in. That nest,
the highest lurch and curve of one branch,
two black birds, who watch in silhouette.

COPLAND SMITH

Arabella

We like to go on bike-rides,
explore deserted houses.
She laughs as every joke glides
as silky as her blouse is
and I would like to do it
with Arabella Hewitt.

She joins us in the garden
for tea, and whispers *salt please*.
Of course, I stammer, 'Pardon.'
She whispers *pass the salt please*
She knows I want to do it
does Arabella Hewitt

We seem to talk for hours
of Plath and Robert Lowell
and when we're caught in showers
I dry her with a towel
and very nearly do it
with Arabella Hewitt.

At uni, off my head.
In love. Exalted. Smitten.
She married Tim, and said
I thought you would have written.
I never did quite do it
with Arabella Hewitt.

CAT P

Ten

taught to lie back and think of England
like I thought other girls do
not yet ten
cling to sheets
feel faint heart beat

it's still me
just
still

taught to lie back and think of England
learnt how to please and do
like Hegel's slave
owned the key
to my escape

taught to lie back and think of England
its okay
my friends have done it too

passion powered
heart soured

taught to lie back and think of England
but I
should
like you

I
should
know
better

Puppywolf and the Night Sky

Puppywolf sits on a rock and stares at the night sky.
Freckles of light spread in a crown above him.
The universe is bigger than Puppywolf.
He knows that.
Sometimes he smells things in the stars.
Shapes, sometimes.
A juicy lump of gristle
or a cute girl puppy.
When he was younger
Puppywolf would yip and jump at the visions,
trying to catch them in his teeth.
No more.
Puppywolf is too smart for that.
Instead he watches, and wonders, and waits.

ANDY N

Final Appointment

I felt the walls
move in like
a tortoise on speed
when you told
me that again.

I could hear
the birds stop singing.

I could hear
cars suddenly stop.

Dogs stop barking
to be let in.

Cats no longer
scratching walls.

Trains no longer making
buildings shake
like a kettle
about to explode.

All I could hear
was my heart
with a faint beat
which was then
skittled down
like a strike
in a bowling alley
when you told me again.

It didn't get any better
on repeated listening.

MARY BRETT

Dream in Ruffles and Lace

Dream in ruffles and lace,
don't stir.
With your hair like a lamb's long fleece,
Rolling over your bosom's white, foamy waves, sleep.
Though mists swirl outside your bedroom lattice,
And above them, the moon looms full.

Dream in ruffles and lace,
just sleep.
Though a dog howls in a yard nearby,
Just breathe, your sweet breath out, don't cry.
Thus shimmer the silver flowers,
Embroidered on your nightgown's froth.

Dream, your peaceful dreams,
While something at your bed's foot stirs.
Relive, watching the swans gliding in the glade;
Lately, your compelled tending of a stranger's grave;
And all your cosy, pretty girlish delights.
A black shape rises at the foot of your bed, but, be calm.
It hovers – huge, and swelling – don't alarm.

Though a bat zig-zags squeaking over your chest,
Moonbeams glint from the cross near your throat.
And soon, the scent of violets fills the air,
and the room lightens, grey fog slipping through the casement,
by your Virgin's altar there.

And, now she's here.
The woman you saw in your dressing-table mirror,
in recent candlelight. Small, slight, with bell-shaped skirt,
Black ringlets glossy by her pallid neck.

A cross is near her throat,
A testament in her hand,
And still, the faint lingering of grave-earth's about her;
White poppies edge her veil.
Perhaps, tonight, you will dream of her.

NEIL BUNDY AND ROBERT AMSBURY

Birthplace – a Code Poem

*(Note: Manchester is widely regarded as the birthplace of the
modern computer, as the 'Baby' – the first stored-program digital
computer – was invented here in 1948. Computer code is itself a
language, which can create all kinds of things when 'spoken'
between computers. The following is a piece of code poetry,
written in Visual Basic. The program helps with communication.)*

```
Public Sub ParseEmail()

  Dim i As Integer
  Dim intTags, intPos, intLen As Integer
  Dim strBoundary As String
  Dim strBuffer As String
  Dim strMsg As String

  strBoundary = modINI.GetEnvVar("Boundary")
  intTags = frmEditTags.fgTags.Rows - 1

  ReDim strData(intTags, 1)
  For i = 1 To (intTags)
    strData(i, 1) = frmEditTags.fgTags.TextMatrix(i, 1)
  Next

  Open strEmailFile For Input As #1

  Do While Not EOF(1)
    Line Input #1, strBuffer

    ReDim Preserve strData(intTags, intBoundaryCount + 1)
    strData(1, intBoundaryCount + 1) = intBoundaryCount

    intBoundaryCount = intBoundaryCount + 1

    Do

      For i = 2 To intTags
```

```
            intPos = InStr(strBuffer, strData(i, 1))

        If intPos = 1 Then
            intLen = Len(strData(i, 1))
            strData(i, intBoundaryCount) = Mid(strBuffer,_
1 + intLen)
            strData(i, intBoundaryCount) = Replace(strData(i,_
intBoundaryCount), vbTab, "")
            strData(i, intBoundaryCount) = Replace(strData(i,_
intBoundaryCount), ",", "")
            Exit For
        End If

    Next i

    Line Input #1, strBuffer

    Loop Until (InStr(strBuffer, strBoundary) > 0)


Loop

intBoundaryCount = intBoundaryCount - 1

Close #1
```

JUSTIN DOOLEY

Fog

Sitting where the darkness paints
itself upon the wall's fiery flickers
he recites tall tales of his sea-spent
days. Living his life through the

eyes of a deckhand who saw the
edge of the Earth, fell off it, returned
in search of a sympathetic ear to
tantalise and was found wanting.

Navigated treacherous horizons
of unfathomable continents,
escaped the typhoon that sought
to seduce lesser men with her

whirlpool gaze and discovered
commodities of indigenous tribes,
bribed with them with smiles and
crossed their palms with poison.

With sulphur-stained fingertips
he sits and knits a slurred fable
for a table that disregards and drinks
themselves oblivious to his feats

of battling bows and arrows with
Bismarck artillery. Ignored, with
a bitter mutter he withdraws back
into the embrace of the shadows.

Lightning Source UK Ltd.
Milton Keynes UK
UKOW04f0714030116

9 780956 581907